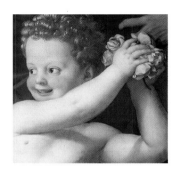

DELIGHT

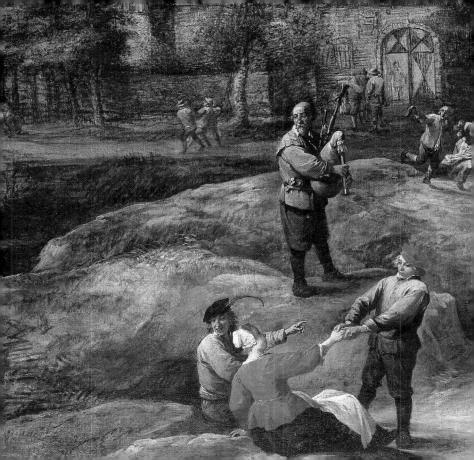

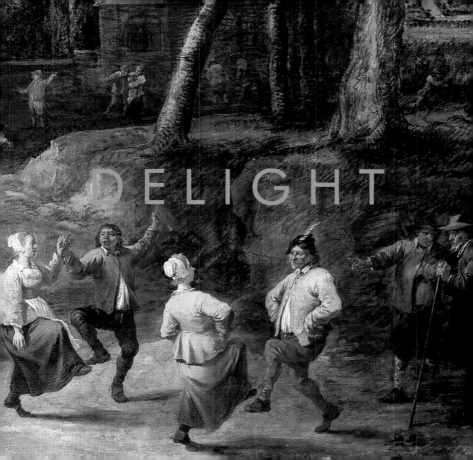

DELIGHT

that moment
of pure
pleasure that
banishes all
pain

from *Song of Pleasure*, Adrian York

this is the garden:colours come and go,
frail azures fluttering from night's
   outer wing
strong silent greens serenely lingering,
absolute lights like baths of golden snow.

from *this is the garden*, E.E. Cummings

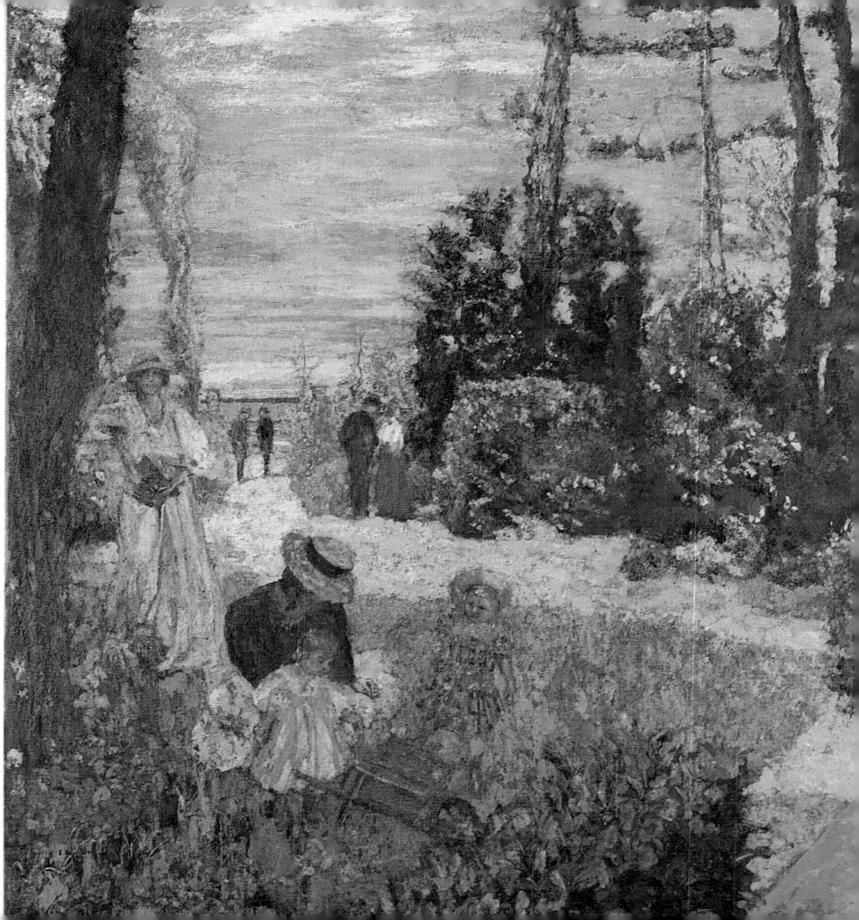

Edouard Vuillard, *Lunch at Vasouy*

colours
come
and go

François Bonvin, *Still Life with Book, Papers and Inkwell*

A precious – mouldering
    pleasure – 'tis –
To meet an Antique Book –
In just the Dress his Century wore –
A privilege – I think –.

A Precious – Mouldering Pleasure – 'Tis, Emily Dickinson

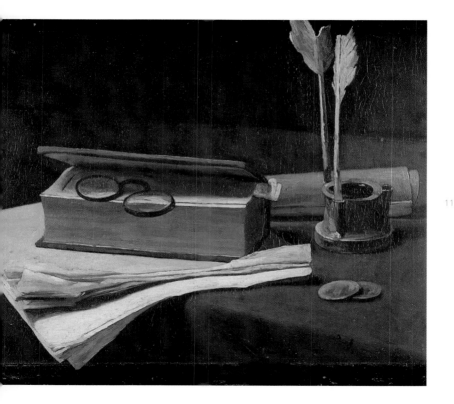

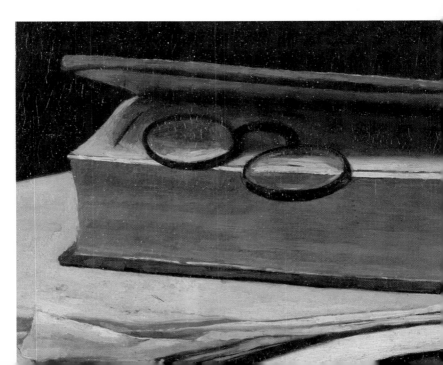

mouldering pleasure

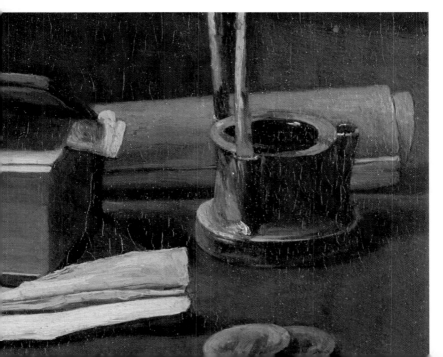

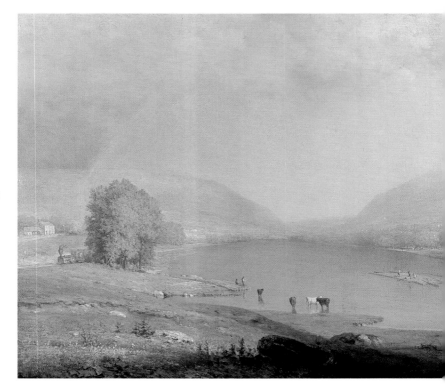

George Inness the Elder, *Delaware Water Gap*

My heart leaps up when
I behold
A rainbow in the sky.

from '*My Heart Leaps up when I Behold*',
William Wordsworth

My heart leaps

18

A sweet disorder in the dress
…Do more bewitch me than when art
Is too precise in every part.

from *Delight in Disorder*, Robert Herrick

sweet disorder

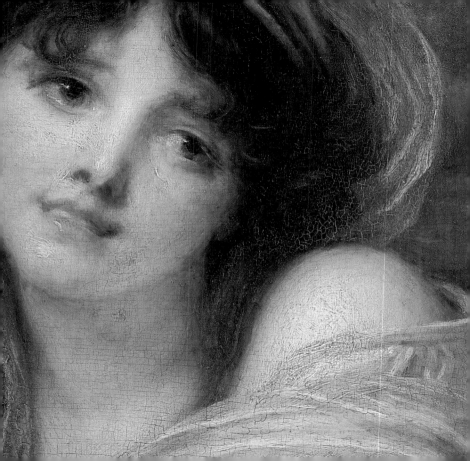

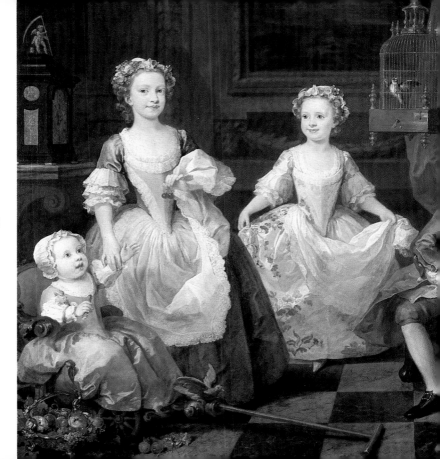

A whisper, then silence:
    Yet I know by their merry eyes
They are plotting and planning
    together
    To take me by surprise.

from *The Children's Hour*, Henry Wadsworth Longfellow

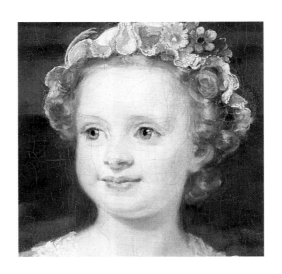

merry eyes

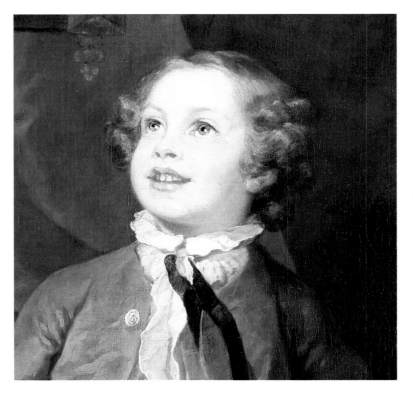

25

So purely, so palely,
Tinily, surely,
Mightily, frailly,
Insculpted and embossed,
With His hammer of wind,
And His graver of frost.

from *To a Snowflake*, Francis Thomson

Alfred Sisley, The Watering Place at Marly-le-Roi

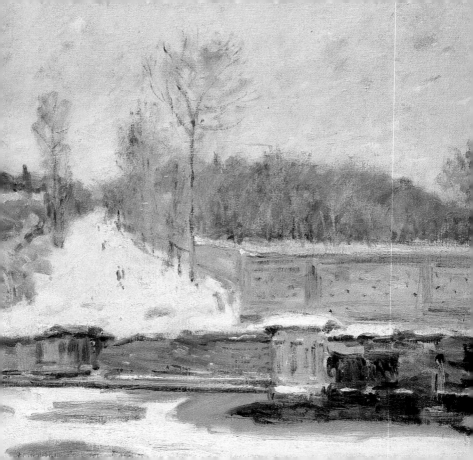

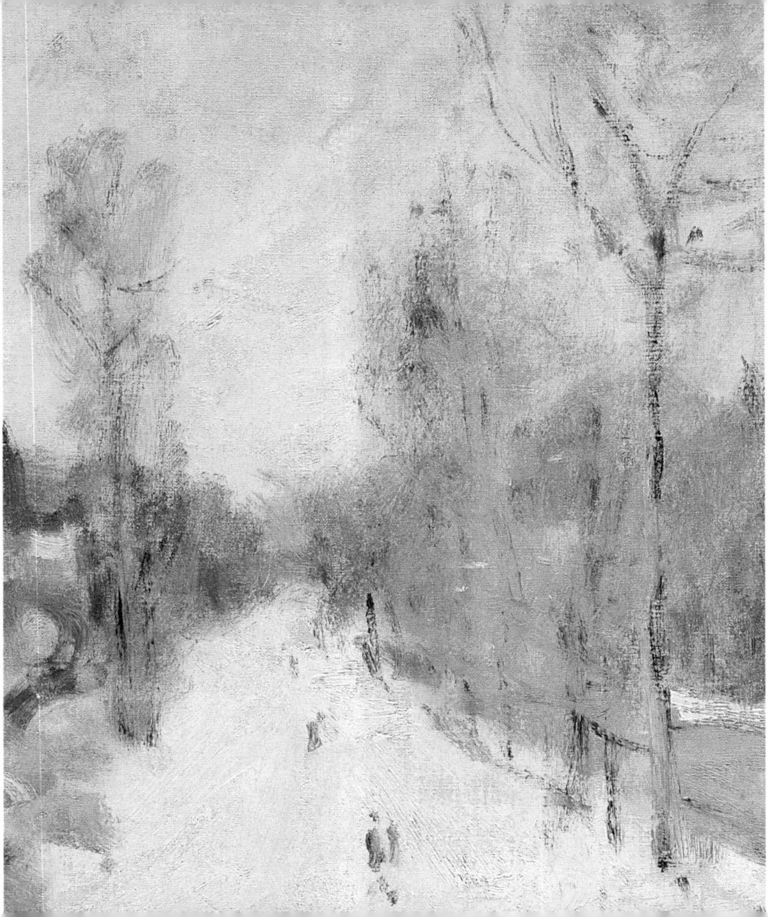

palely,
Tinily, surely

"A loaf of bread," the Walrus said
"Is what we chiefly need:
Pepper and vinegar besides
Are very good indeed –
Now, if you're ready Oysters dear,
We can begin to feed."

from *The Walrus and the Carpenter*, Lewis Carroll

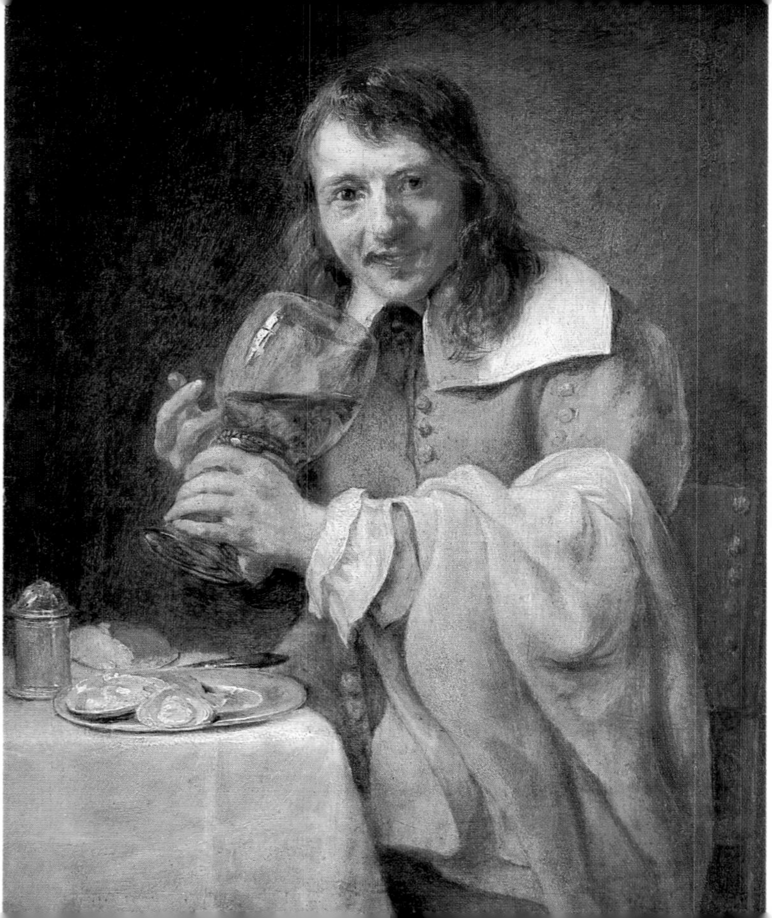

After Coques, *Taste*

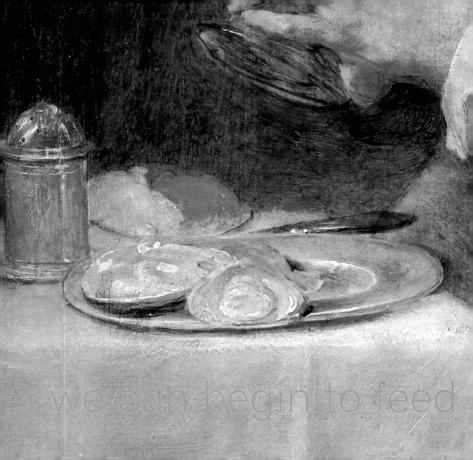

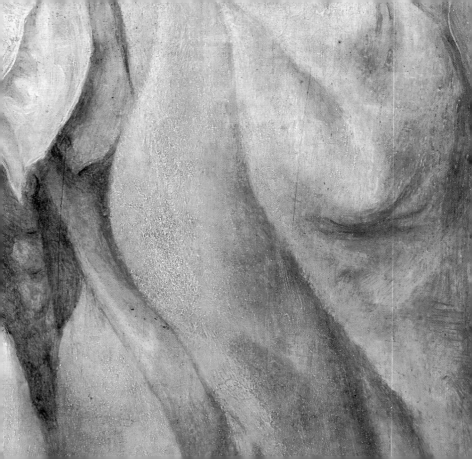

Imitator of Jongkind, *Skating in Holland*

Skaters on the pond vanish
In dusk, but their voices stay,
Calling and laughing

from *Like Queen Christina*, Kenneth Rexroth

calling and laughing

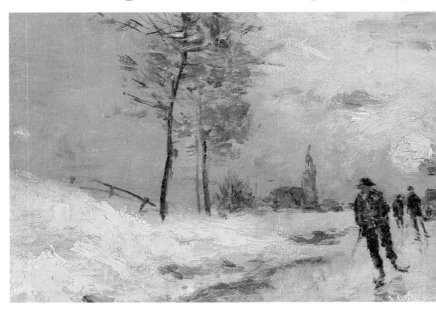

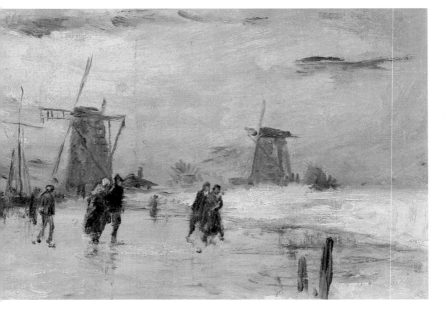

Happy those early days! when I
Shined in my angel infancy

from *The Retreat*, Henry Vaughan

Federico Barocci, *The Madonna and Child with Saint Joseph and the Infant Baptist (La Madonna del Gatto)*

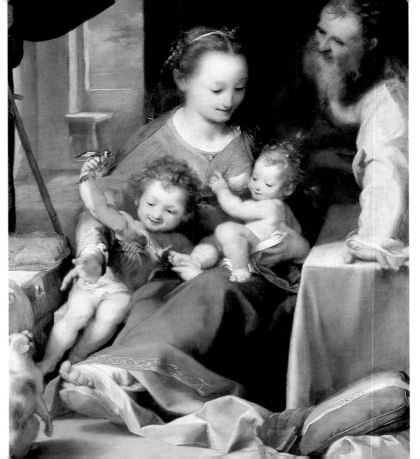

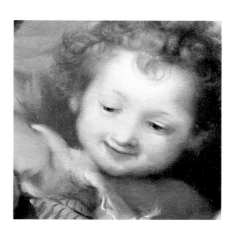

Happy
those
early
days!

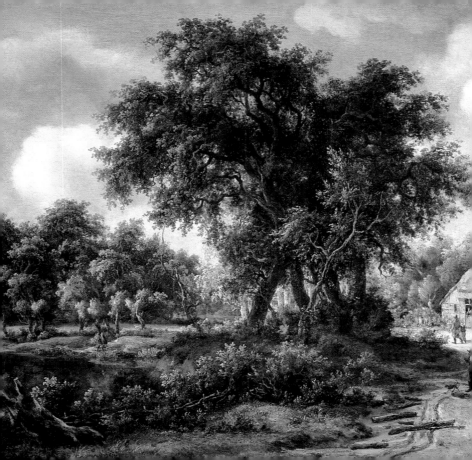

I remember,
    I remember
The house where
    I was born,
The little window
    where the sun
Came peeping in
    at morn

from *Past and Present*, Thomas Hood

43

the house
where I was
born

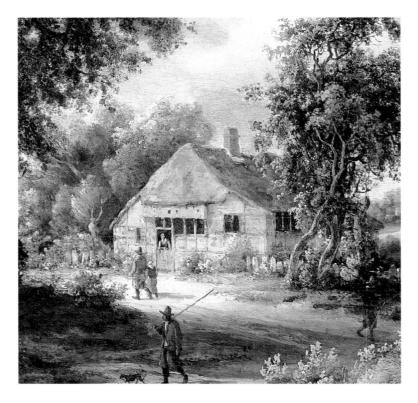

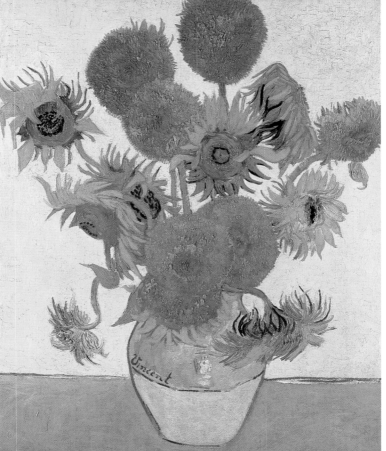

Vincent van Gogh, *Sunflowers*

Bring me the sunflower,
madly in love with light.

from *The Sunflower*, Eugenio Montale

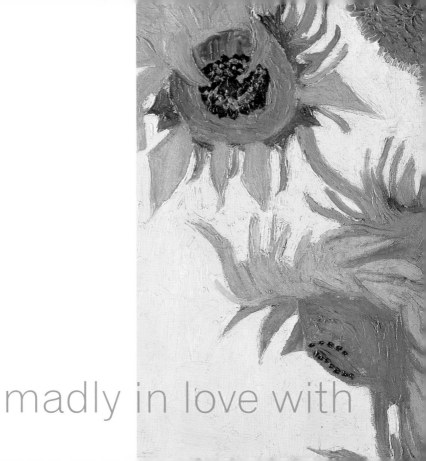

madly in love with

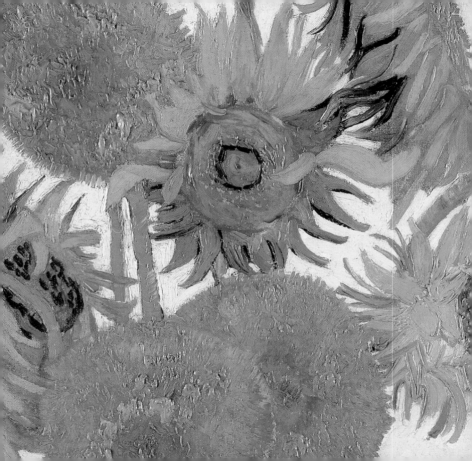

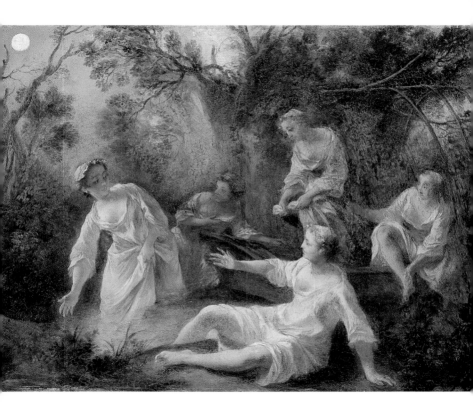

Angel spirits of sleep,
White-robed, with silver hair,
In your meadows fair,
Where the willows weep,
And the sad moonbeam
On the gliding stream
Writes her scatter'd dream.

from *Spirits*, Robert Bridges

51

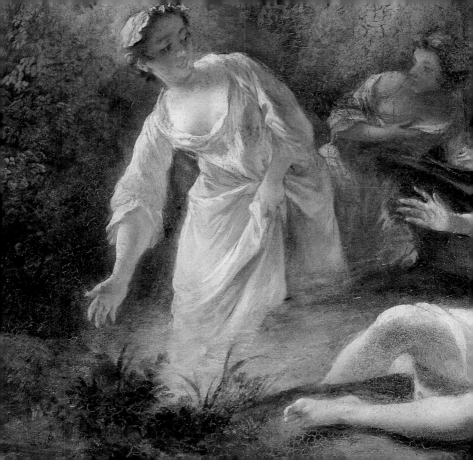

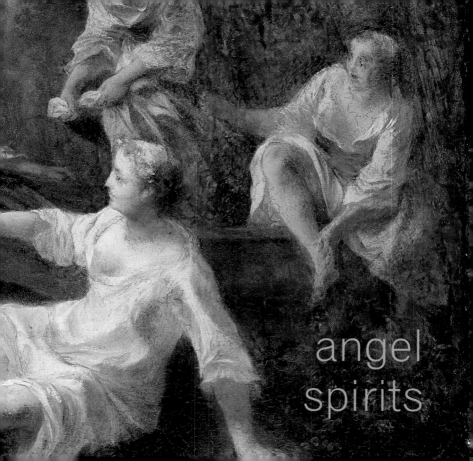

angel
spirits

But I am done with apple-picking now.
Essence of winter sleep is on the night,
The scent of apples: I am drowsing off.

from *After Apple-Picking*, Robert Frost

Jean-Désiré-Gustave Courbet, *Still Life with Apples and a Pomegranate*

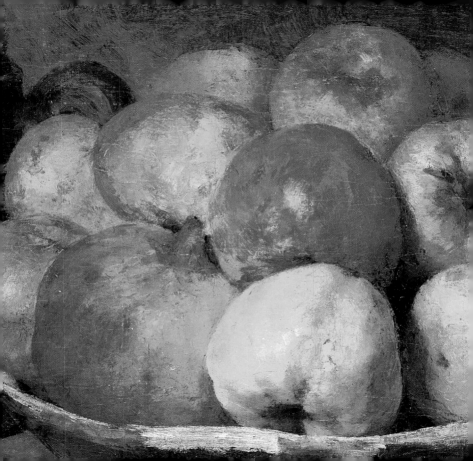

scent of apples

Nicolas Poussin, *The Triumph of Pan*

These violent delights have violent ends.

from *Romeo and Juliet*, William Shakespeare

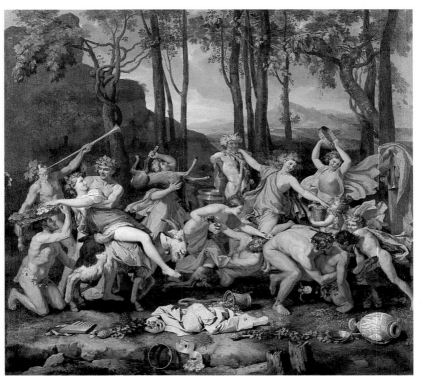

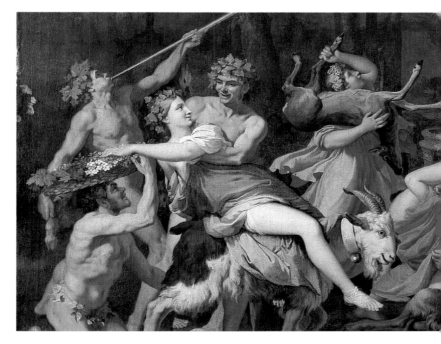

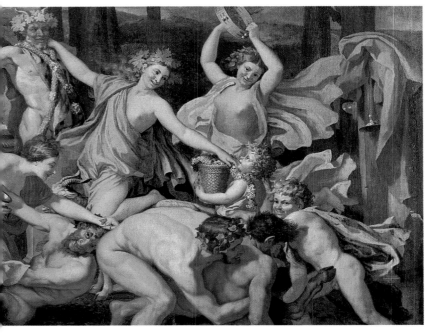

violent delight

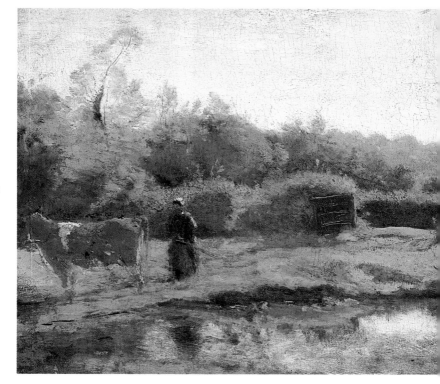

Jean-Baptiste-Camille Corot, *Summer Morning*

Very early in the morning
    sunlight runs
Plucking at the grass
    blades with the spheres'
    music,
And the silver-candled
    moon in the dawn
Kindles in each dewdrop a
    reflected song.

from *The Seasons*, M.L., a nun of Burnham Abbey

morning sunlight

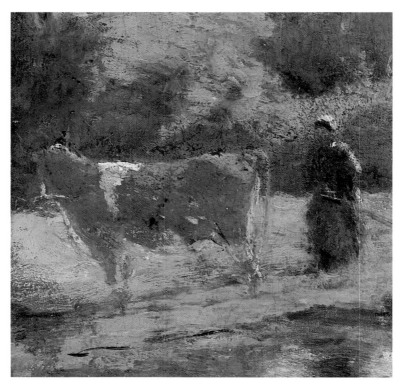

Thomas Gainsborough, *The Painter's Daughters chasing a Butterfly*

Today a butterfly froze in midair;
and was plucked like a grape by a child
who swore he could take care of it.

from *The Wheelchair Butterfly*, James Tate

a butterfly froze

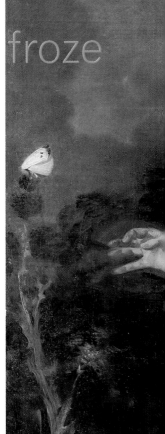

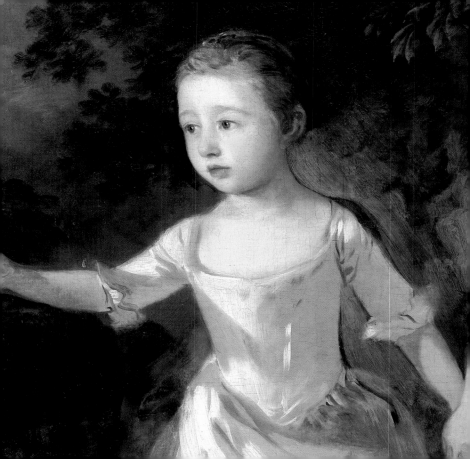

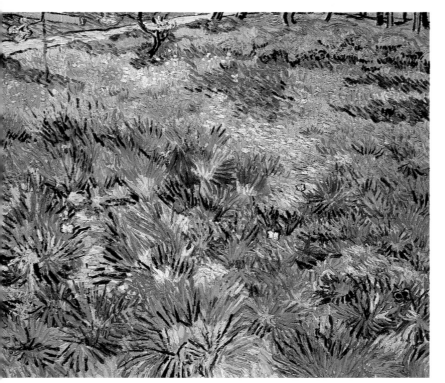

When weeds in wheels, shoot long and
    lovely and lush;
Thrush's eggs look little low heavens

from *Spring*, Gerard Manley Hopkins

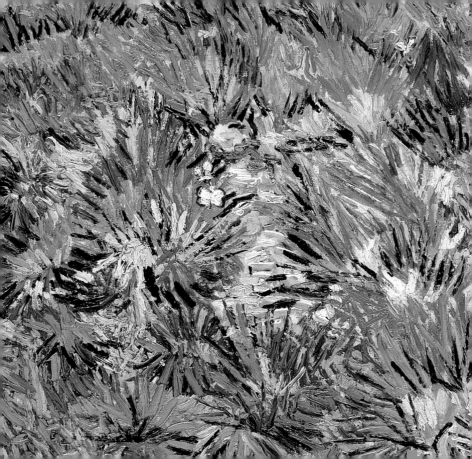

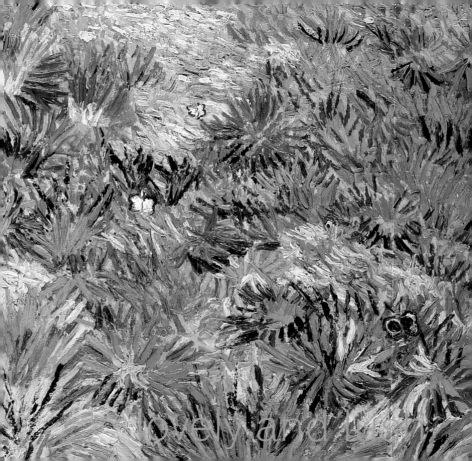

Follower of Leonardo, *Narcissus*

And when she balanced in the
    delight of her thought,
A wren, happy, tail to the wind

from *Elegy for Jane*, Theodore Roethke

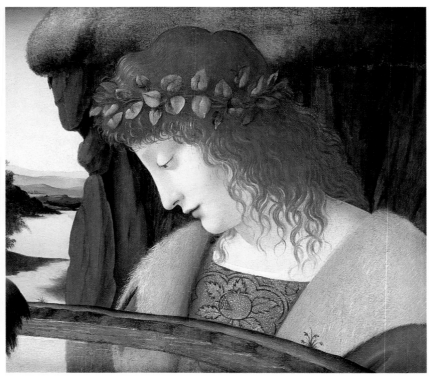

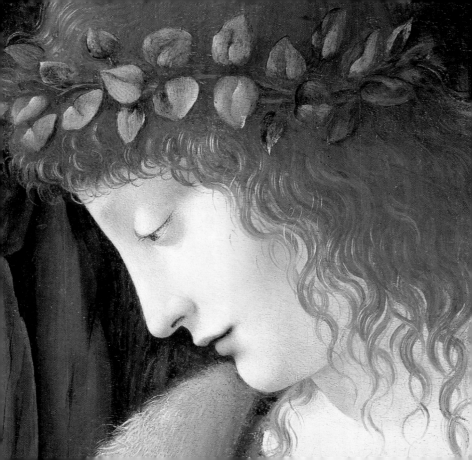

balanced in
the delight of
her thought

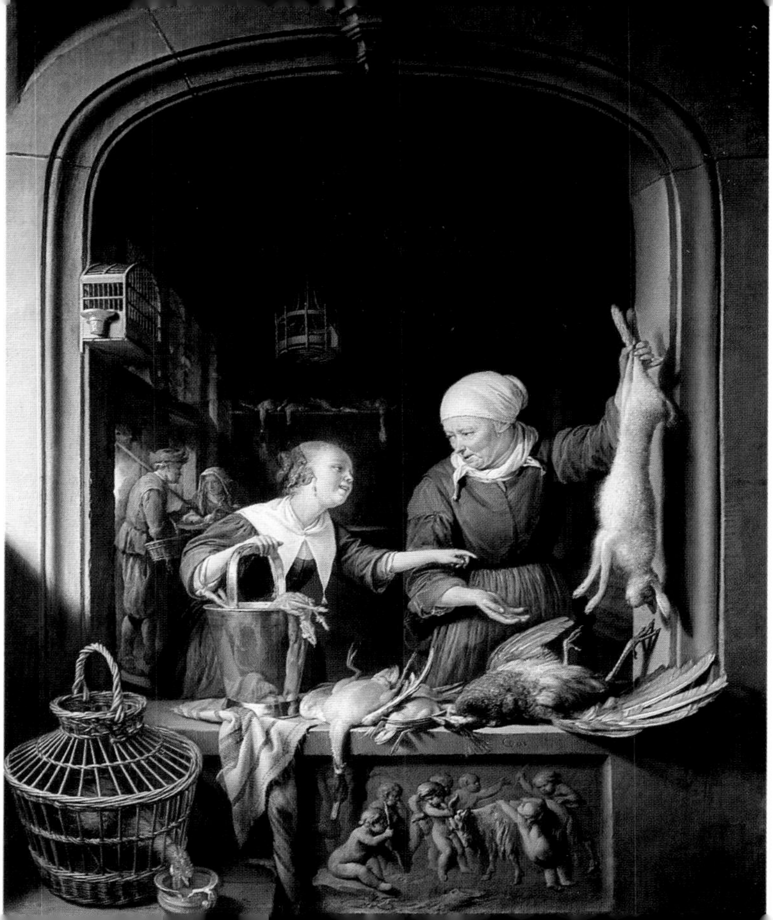

Gerrit Dou, *A Poulterer's Shop*

I came to buy a smile – today –
But just a single smile –
The smallest one upon your face
Will suit me just as well –

from *I Came to Buy a Smile*, Emily Dickinson

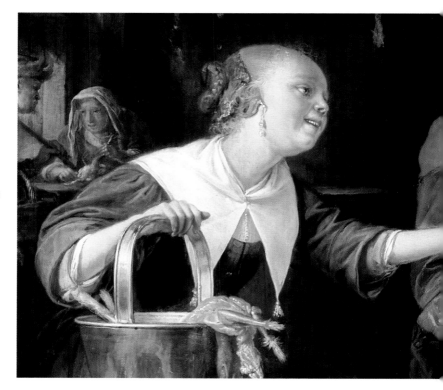

80

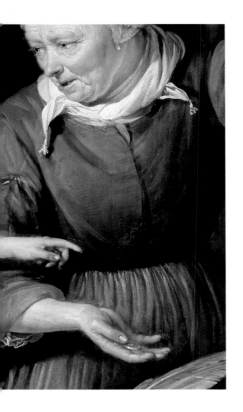

I came
to buy
a smile

I was a child and overwhelmed: Mozart
Had snatched me up fainting and wild at heart
To a green land of wonder

from *The Corner Knot*, Robert Graves

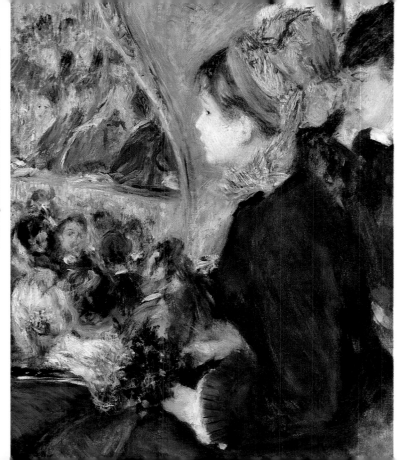

Pierre-Auguste Renoir, *At the Theatre (La Première Sortie)*

83

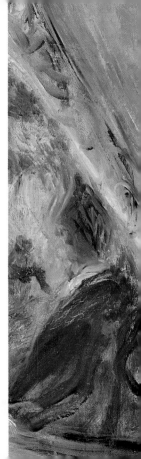

I was a child
and
overwhelmed

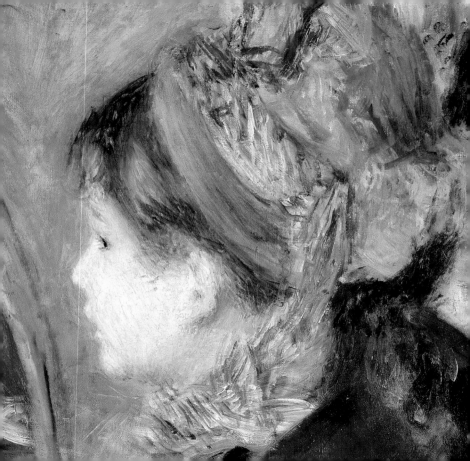

I will get a new string for my fiddle,
  And call to the neighbours to come,
And partners shall dance down the middle
  Until the old pewter-wares hum:
  And we'll sip the mead, cyder, and rum!

from *A Merry-making in Question*, Thomas Hardy

Lucas van Uden, *Peasants merry-making before a Country House*

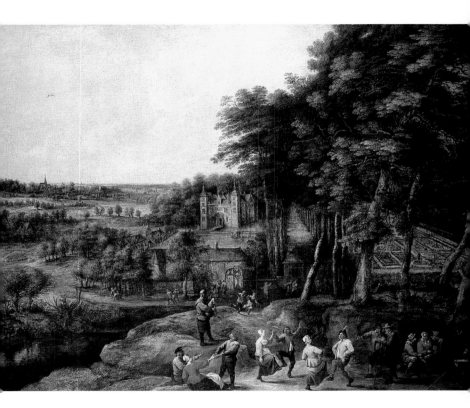

and

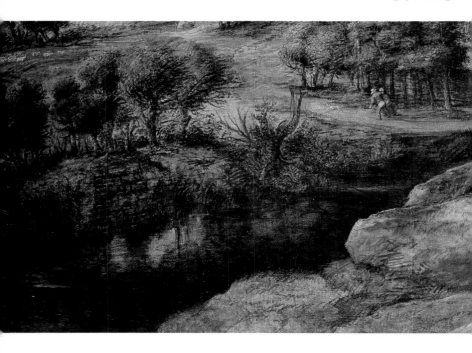

partners shall dance

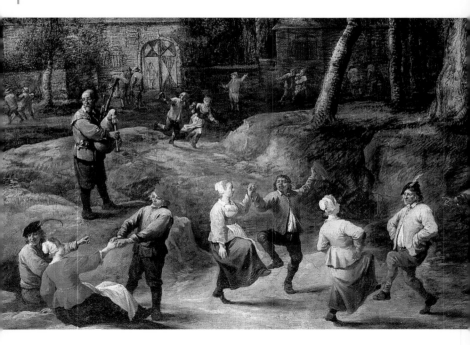

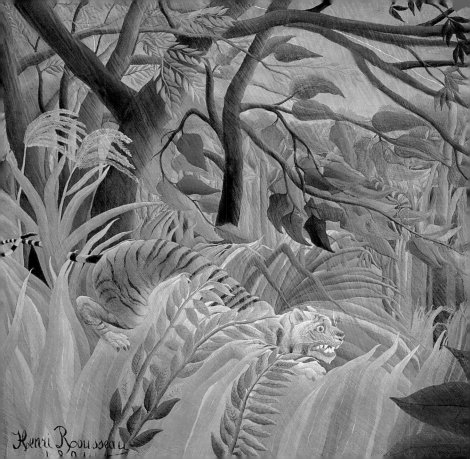

Henri Rouosseau

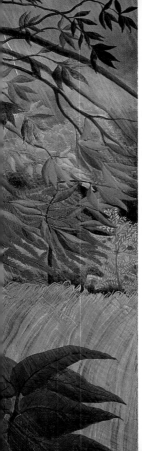

Henri Rousseau, *Tiger in a Tropical Storm (Surprised!)*

The grass is flaming and the
    trees are growing,
The very mud is gurgling in
    the pools,
Green toads are watching,
    crimson parrot flying,
Two pairs of eyes meet one
    another glowing –
They hunt the velvet tigers in
    the jungle.

from *India*, W.J. Turner

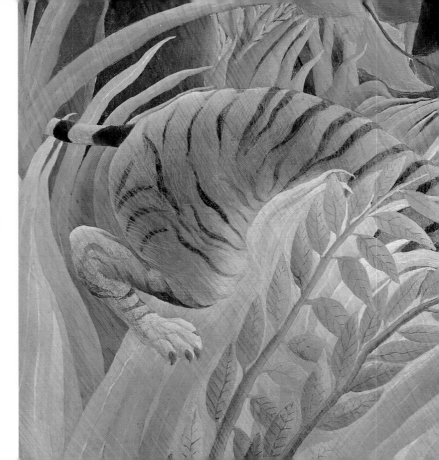

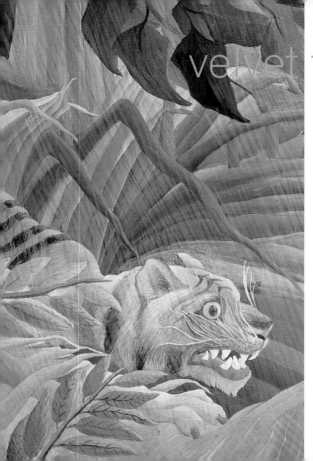

velvet tigers

This Life, which seems so fair,
Is like a bubble blown up in the air,
By sporting children's breath.
Who chase it every where

from *This Life, which Seems so Fair,*
William Drummond of Hawthornden

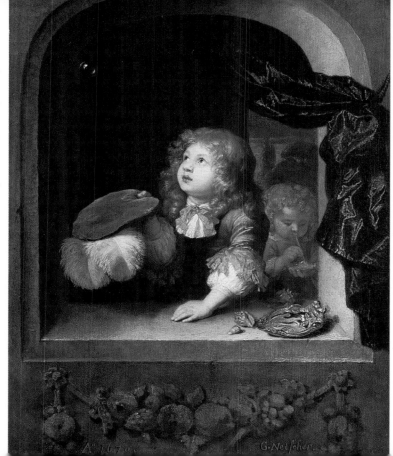

Caspar Netscher, *Two Boys blowing Bubbles*

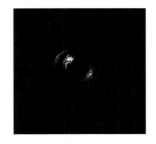

like a
bubble
blown up
in the air

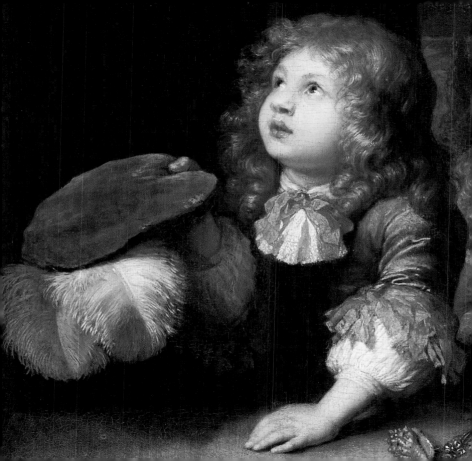

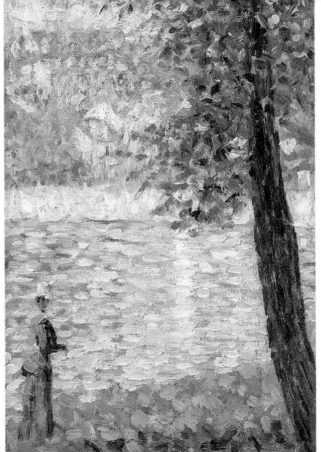

Georges-Pierre Seurat, *The Morning Walk*

For skies as coupe-coloured as a
    brindled cow;
For rose-moles all in stipple upon
    trout that swim

from *Pied Beauty*, Gerard Manley Hopkins

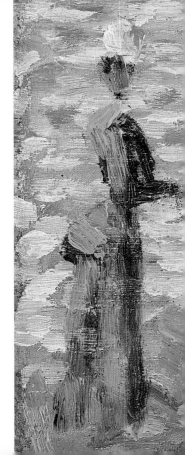

all in stipple

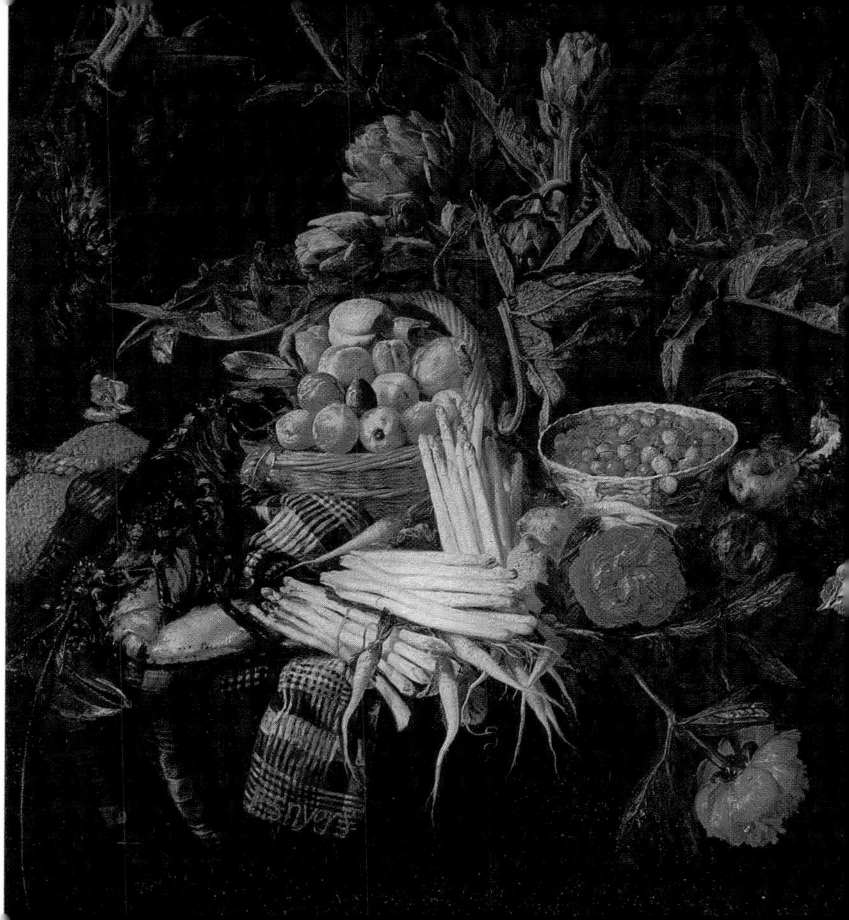

Pieter Snijers, *A Still Life with Fruit, Vegetables, Dead Chickens and a Lobster*

Come buy, come buy:
Apples and quinces
Lemons and oranges,
Plump unpecked cherries
Melons and raspberries
Bloom-down cheeked peaches,
Swart-headed mulberries,
Wild free-born cranberries,
Crab-apples, dew-berries,
Pine-apples, blackberries,
Apricots, strawberries –
All ripe together

from *Goblin Market*, Christina G. Rossetti

bloom-down
cheeked peaches

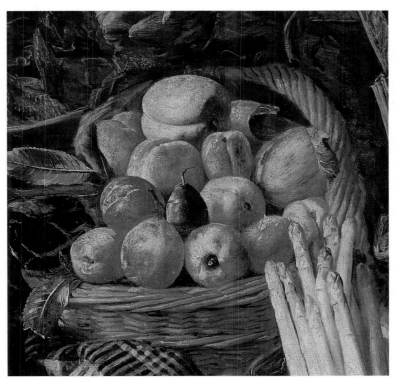

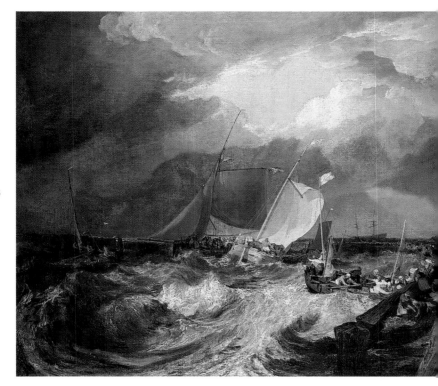

Joseph Mallord Turner, *Calais Pier: An English Packet Arriving*

What's there, beyond? A thing
   unsearch'd and strange;
Not happier, but different.
Something vast
And new. Some unimaginable
   change
From what has been.
Perchance the end at last?

from *Seaward*, Edward Robert Bulwer Lytton

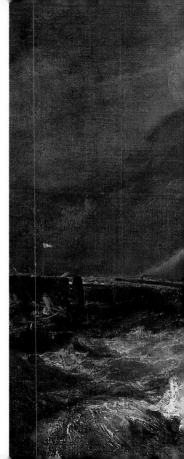

something
vast
and new

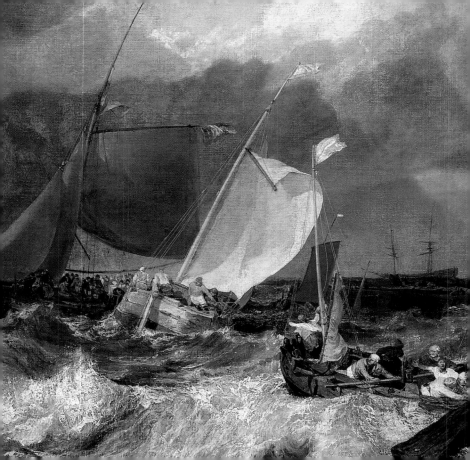

ACKNOWLEDGEMENTS

The editor and publisher gratefully acknowledge permission to reprint the copyright material below. Every effort has been made to contact the original copyright holders of material used. In the case of any accidental infringements, concerned parties are asked to contact the publisher.

The stanza from *this is the garden:colours come and go* is reprinted from *Complete Poems 1904–1962*, by E.E. Cummings, edited by George J. Firmage, by permission of W.W. Norton and Company. Copyright © 1991 by the Trustees for the E.E. Cummings Trust and George James Firmage.

After Apple-Picking by Robert Frost reprinted by permission of Henry Holt & Co., LLC. *The Corner Knot* by Robert Graves from *Complete Poems,* 1997. Reproduced by permission of Carcanet Press Ltd.

INDEX OF PAINTINGS

Published by MQ Publications, Ltd.
254-258 Goswell Road, London EC1V 7RL
in association with National Gallery Company Ltd.

Series Editor: Ljiljana Ortolja-Baird
Designer: Bet Ayer

A CIP catalogue record for this book is available
from the British Library

ISBN: 1 84072 134 0

Printed in Italy

D1270116